A Citizen's Guide to

Governing the UK

Ivan Minnis
Revised and updated by Stewart Ross

Heinemann

www.heinemann.co.uk/library
visit our website to find out more information about **Heinemann Library** books.

To order:
☎ Phone 44 (0) 1865 888112

📄 Send a fax to 44 (0) 1865 314091

💻 Visit the Heinemann Bookshop at www.heinemann.co.uk/library to browse our catalogue and order online.

First published in Great Britain by Heinemann Library, Halley Court, Jordan Hill, Oxford OX2 8EJ, part of Harcourt Education.
Heinemann is a registered trademark of Harcourt Education Ltd.

Design: M2 Graphic Design
Originated by Ambassador Litho Ltd.
Printed in China by WKT Company Ltd.

10 digit ISBN 0 431 06170 X
13 digit ISBN 978 0 431 06170 2

10 09 08 07 06
10 9 8 7 6 5 4 3 2 1

British Library Cataloguing in Publication Data
Minnis, Ivan
  A citizen's guide to tgoverning the UK. - 2nd ed.
  1.Great Britain - Politics and government - 1945- -
Juvenile literature
  I.Title II.Governing the UK
  320.4'41

A full catalogue record for this book is available from the British Library.

Acknowledgements
The publishers would like to thank the following for permission to reproduce photographs:
Courtesy of Foster and Partners/Richard Davies p21; © Hulton-Deutsch Collection/Corbis p9; The *Independent*/David Rose p24, John Voos p17, 26; PA News p12; Popperfoto/Reuters p15, 31, 37; © Reuters Newmedia Inc/Corbis p10, 34, 38; Rex Features Limited p18, 24, 32, 40; Stefan Rousseau/PA Photos p42; The Royal Collection © 2001/Her Majesty Queen Elizabeth p7; Stone/David Oliver p4, Stuart McClymont p23.
The political party symbols used on pages 28-29 are courtesy of the Conservative Party, the Green Party, the Labour Party and the LibDem Party.

Cover photograph of Tony Blair, reproduced with permission of Getty Images/AFP.

Every effort has been made to contact copyright holders of any material reproduced in this book. Any omissions will be rectified in subsequent printings if notice is given to the publishers.
The paper used to print this book comes from sustainable resources.

CONTENTS

Government and you

How our government has developed

Parts of government

Democracy in action

Regional variations

Debate

Any words appearing in the text in bold, **like this**, are explained in the Glossary.

PART 1

GOVERNMENT AND YOU
What is the United Kingdom?

The full title of the United Kingdom or UK is 'the United Kingdom of Great Britain and Northern Ireland.' This shows that the UK is not just one country. Instead it is made up of four nations – England, Scotland, Wales and Northern Ireland, all coming together under one **government**.

Who are the British people?

The term 'British' is used to describe the roughly 59 million inhabitants of the United Kingdom. The table below shows what percentages of people live in each of the four parts of the United Kingdom.

The people of the UK come from a wide variety of **ethnic** and cultural backgrounds. As well as the four nationalities of the British Isles, over three million of us are part of a non-white ethnic minority. This means that Britain is a **multi-cultural** state, able to learn from the experiences and cultures of people from all around the world. The wide range of different people in the UK adds to this range of experience. City and country dwellers, old and young, rich and poor – all of us have a role to play in the development and government of the country.

The percentage of the population from each part of the UK.*

COUNTRY	POPULATION (MILLIONS)	POPULATION (%)
ENGLAND	49.8	83.7
SCOTLAND	5.0	8.5
WALES	2.9	4.9
NORTHERN IRELAND	1.7	2.9
UK TOTAL	59.4	100

*Source: National Statistical Office, 2003

Electing our leaders

How often have you heard someone say what they would do if they were running the country or their local council? People are always complaining about **politicians**, but sometimes forget that it is the people of the UK who elect these politicians, and we can vote them out of power if we do not like what they say or do.

In June 2005, the people of the UK re-elected the Labour government. All British **citizens** who were eighteen years old or over were entitled to vote, deciding which party they felt should run the country, and rewarding them with power. Yet only just over 60 per cent of these people voted, and fewer than half of them voted for the **party** that won. This meant that the new government, elected with a large majority of seats in **parliament**, received the support of only around one quarter of the population overall. Turnout for council elections is even lower, so next time you hear someone complain about politicians, ask what they are doing to change things!

Making a difference

There are around eight million teenagers across the United Kingdom. Unable to vote, many under-eighteens feel that politics is not for them, but there are many ways in which you can help to change society. Here are just some of them:

>> Join a political party: all of the major political parties encourage young people to join, hoping that they will help to shape the politics of the future.

>> Influence local politicians: local authorities often have youth councils that allow young people to have their say in improving community facilities.

>> Join a pressure group: if you believe strongly in a cause, these allow you to help make politicians listen to your opinions.

>> Write a letter: it may sound simple, but letters and petitions sent to politicians and newspapers often make those in power take notice of people's opinions.

Throughout this book you will find other ways of getting involved, as well as web addresses that will help you to find the information you need to get started.

A school united

How would you feel if you found out that one of your friends was going to be forced to leave the country? This is happening around Britain, as families hoping to gain **asylum** in this country have their cases rejected by the **Home Office**. When staff and pupils at Forest Gate School in London learned that one of the students was to be sent back to Angola, they launched a campaign to keep her in the UK. They were able to draw in the media, forcing the Home Office first to delay the deportation, and then to allow the girl's family to stay.

The Institute of Race Relations has set up a website to help schools in this position. The Schools against Deportations site can be found at www.irr.org.uk/sad/.

PART 2

HOW OUR GOVERNMENT HAS DEVELOPED
The origins of the British Parliament

After the Norman Conquest of 1066, **monarchs** ruled like **dictators**. In order to maintain their power, they relied on an oath of loyalty sworn by noblemen. In exchange for this oath of loyalty, the monarchs gave land to their supporters and the church.

This system began to change during the reign of King John (1199–1216). John angered his noblemen by bringing in high **taxation**. They rose up against him, forcing him to agree to a series of demands, set out in the Magna Carta of 1215. This document was the first in a series that gradually introduced new powers to the Great Council. Kings were forced to call the Great Council's members if they wanted to introduce new taxes. The Council began to meet more regularly, and the first **Parliament** was born.

Lords and Commons

In medieval times, many European rulers worked with some kind of parliament. In England it consisted of two chambers, an upper house – the Lords, and a lower – the Commons. At first the Lords, the great landowners and churchmen, gathered to advise the King. This changed in the thirteenth century. The Lords said they could only agree to taxes on behalf of those who worked on their land. At the same time, the king found it sensible to hear what knights from the shires and burgesses from the towns thought of his policies. In 1264, the first 'Commons' gathering of shire knights was summoned, soon joined by burgesses. Within 150 years it was accepted that the Commons has supremacy over the Lords in matters regarding taxation.

Who should rule, Crown or Commons?

In the sixteenth century, the Tudors altered the country's religion through Parliament. Lords and Commons were now involved in two key policy areas: taxation and religion. After Charles I (1625–1649) had clashed with parliaments over both these issues, he refused to call parliaments for eleven years. Financial necessity forced him to back down, and by 1642 King and Parliament were engaged in a **civil war**.

Charles was defeated in England and Scotland, and the English army put him on trial for treason – acting against the wishes and interests of his people. He was found guilty and beheaded in 1649. From then on, no monarch would be able to rule without heeding the wishes of his or her more influential subjects.

The restoration of the monarchy and the 'Glorious Revolution'

For eleven years England was without a king. Parliament's attempts to rule alone ended in failure. In 1660, the executed king's son was invited to return to take the throne as Charles II. However, religious tensions remained high. Charles' heir, James, was a **Catholic**, and as Charles II grew older, many **Protestants** in England began to fear that they would be persecuted when James became king.

James' reign lasted only three years. In 1688, a group of Protestant noblemen, paranoid at the king's religious and political intentions, invited his Protestant daughter Mary and her Dutch husband, Prince William of Orange, to replace him. This 'Glorious and Bloodless Revolution' was carried out so that a monarch could never again act contrary to the wishes of Parliament.

Parliament takes control

The reign of William III and Mary II (1688–1702) confirmed Parliament's new role in British government. A **Bill of Rights** said that elections were to be free and Members of Parliament (MPs) were to have freedom of speech and debate. Monarchs were not to tax, raise an army or alter the law without parliamentary consent. Parliament met regularly too, in order to vote in the heavy taxation needed for William's anti-Catholic

wars. Britain was still a long way from being a democracy, but its balanced government at least guaranteed that, from now on, the views of Parliament would be heard.

Prince William of Orange, ruler of Holland, lands in England on 5 November 1688.

A United Kingdom?

When Elizabeth I died in 1603 leaving no heir, Scotland's King James VI became also King James I of England, Wales and Ireland. His realm was by no means united, though. Wales had been invaded by England in the twelfth century and had gradually become part of the English political system, but Ireland and Scotland had their own parliaments. It was not until the 1707 Act of Union that the Scottish parliament voted itself out of existence, and instead began to send MPs to London. Ireland kept its own parliament until the Act of Union of 1801 created the United Kingdom of Great Britain and Ireland. This remained unchanged until 1922, when a war for independence in Ireland led to the creation of the Irish Free State, leaving only the six counties of Northern Ireland within the UK.

HOW OUR GOVERNMENT HAS DEVELOPED
The move towards democracy

While debating whether James II should be allowed to become king, **MPs** split into two loose **parties**, called the Whigs and the Tories (see pages 26–29). Later changing their names, these two groups dominated politics for the next 200 years. **Monarchs** still chose their own **ministers**, although these had to have parliamentary backing. The leading ministers formed the **Cabinet**. William III and Anne (1702–1714) preferred a cabinet of Tory ministers but accepted Whigs. To avoid a Catholic monarch, in 1714 the Whigs invited a German Protestant, George of Hanover, to the throne. As a result, George relied on a cabinet that was exclusively Whig and its leading figure, Robert Walpole, became the first prime minister.

A corrupt system

Although some of our modern political terms were coming into use, politics was very different from today. Elections were often corrupt, with 'rotten' and 'pocket' boroughs common. In 'rotten' boroughs, MPs were said to bribe their way to election, while in 'pocket' boroughs, the MP was chosen by a tiny, easily manipulated group of electors. Thus the borough was said to be 'in the pocket' of a powerful patron. There were no consistent rules as to who could vote – in some **constituencies** it depended on how much you earned, and in others on the size of your fireplace!

Parliamentary reform

By the late eighteenth century, Britain was changing rapidly. The Industrial Revolution was causing an explosion in the number of people living in towns. A new 'middle class' of wealthy businessmen was emerging, mainly living in the new industrial cities. This rich and powerful group felt the electoral system did not represent them fairly in parliament. Change eventually came in 1832, when the Great Reform Act transferred 150 seats from 'rotten' boroughs to the growing towns. However, it was generally still only the well-off who had the right to vote – there were only 650,000 voters out of a population of eighteen million.

The extension of the franchise

Parliament had passed the 1832 Reform Act because it feared unrest. Nevertheless, the calls for reform had not been silenced. **Radicals** challenged the right of just the wealthy to vote, many demanding **universal suffrage** – the right for all men to vote. The 1867 Reform Act extended the franchise, or the right to vote, to around 30 per cent of adult men. The 1884 Act raised that figure to 40 per cent. Even so, most working-class men and all women still could not vote.

Changing attitudes, speeded up by the First World War, led to further reform. Women had taken over the jobs of the men fighting in the war, and when it ended in 1918, the **government** felt obliged to grant these women the vote. Likewise, the thousands of working class men who had suffered in the trenches 'for King and Country' could not be refused a say in the government of their country.

In 1918, the Representation of the People Act gave the vote in parliamentary elections to all men over 21 and to women over 30. This age difference was removed in 1928. Further changes followed, until the 1969 Act eventually lowered the voting age for all to eighteen. Over 150 years since the 1832 Reform Act had increased the **electorate** to 650,000, 40 million men and women now had the vote. Universal suffrage had finally been achieved.

Votes for women!

The Industrial Revolution had seen thousands of women enter the workforce, while universities were beginning to accept female students. As the nineteenth century drew to a close, both women and men were questioning a system that accepted women's contribution to the country's success, but would not allow them to vote for its government. In 1903, Emmeline Pankhurst founded the Women's Social and Political Union to demand a change to this system.

The protests of the 'Suffragettes', as they became known, shocked society. Many members who were imprisoned for damage to property went on hunger **strike** in prison. One Suffragette, Emily Davison, was killed when she threw herself under the King's horse at the Derby horse race in a bid to highlight her cause. Despite the outrage generated by such actions, the Suffragettes kept their cause in the public eye. Cessation of trouble-making on the outbreak of war in 1914, and their strong support for the war effort, helped produce the 1918 Representation of the People Act.

This gave women the right to vote, but only those over 30. In 1928, women finally gained the same voting rights as men.

Women and their supporters take to the streets of London in 1913 demanding the right to vote.

PARTS OF GOVERNMENT
The constitution and the monarchy

The **constitution** of a country is the set of rules by which it is governed. In most countries this is a written document that explains and limits the role of each branch of **government**, and guarantees the **rights** of the ordinary **citizen**. For a new law to be introduced it must be constitutional (within the rules of the country). If not, it can be challenged in court.

Britain does not have a written constitution, or any single document that can be used to challenge new laws. Instead the British constitution has evolved over centuries and is made up of a variety of documents:

>> At its centre is Statute Law, laws relating to the constitution. In 1998, Parliament passed the Government of Wales Act, setting up the Welsh Assembly. As this changed how we are governed, the Act has become part of the constitution.

>> International **treaties** can also make changes. When Britain signed the Treaty of Rome and joined the European Community (EC) in 1973, the treaty was incorporated into the British constitution because Parliament had handed over some power to the EC.

>> The constitution also includes conventions. These are rules of government that have become accepted over many years of use. For example, it is accepted that while

The Queen and Prince Philip arrive for the formal opening of Parliament. The British constitution has many traditions like this.

the **monarch** must give **royal assent** to a **bill** for it to become law, it would be unconstitutional for them not to do so. No monarch has refused since 1708.

>> Parliamentary sovereignty is at the centre of the constitution; Parliament is the supreme authority in the land. Under this authority, Parliament could vote to withdraw from the EU or dissolve the Welsh Assembly, removing them from the constitution.

In most countries with a written constitution, the rules remain in place until a **referendum** is held. Supporters of the British system argue that it is flexible, allowing the constitution to change with the times. Opponents fear it allows Parliament to change laws as it pleases, and fails to protect the rights of the individual.

The monarchy

Britain is very different from most modern **democracies** in that it is a monarchy. In France and the USA, the people elect the **head of state** – the President. In Britain the head of state is the monarch – the king or queen. The monarch is not elected by the people; instead the position is inherited. When the present queen dies, she will be replaced by her son, Prince Charles, who in turn will be replaced by his heir.

The political role of the monarchy

The monarch has limited powers within the British system of government:

>> Dissolution of Parliament: before a **General Election** can be called, the outgoing Prime Minister must ask the monarch to dissolve Parliament.

>> Royal assent: in order for a piece of **legislation** to become law, it must be signed by the monarch.

>> Appointing Prime Ministers: after a General Election, the monarch asks one of the **party** leaders to form the government and become Prime Minister.

>> The Queen's Speech: the government is called 'Her Majesty's Government'. At the start of each **parliamentary session**, the Queen opens Parliament and reads a speech that sets out the government's proposed legislation for that session.

>> Head of state: the monarch plays an important role in representing Britain overseas as head of state, especially within the **Commonwealth**.

Why do we still have a monarchy?

Most democracies are **republics**. They do not have a monarch. Instead, they elect a President as their head of state. The powers of these leaders vary greatly. In Ireland, the President has little power, while the President of the USA is often described as the most powerful person in the world.

In Britain, the monarch is not a member of any political group, and is even banned from voting. Many people feel that this allows the monarch to represent the people without thinking of political gain. In times of crisis, such as during the Second World War, the monarchy can play an important role in uniting the people. Despite this, the past 20 years has seen a growing campaign for Britain to abolish the monarchy and become a republic.

PARTS OF GOVERNMENT
The Prime Minister and the government

The role of the Prime Minister has changed greatly since the title was first used in the early eighteenth century. Back then, the monarch chose all the ministers, including the Prime Minister, and each was responsible for a different area of government. As **democracy** extended during the nineteenth century, the monarch ceased to have a role in choosing the Cabinet, with the Prime Minister instead appointing senior figures within his own **party**. Gradually, the role of the Prime Minister and the Cabinet grew, and by the beginning of the 20th century, they had become the most important part of political decision making in the country.

What powers does the Prime Minister have?

In June 2005, the people of the UK elected a new **government**. As leader of the victorious Labour Party, Tony Blair became Prime Minster for a third term. In this position he has many powers, but does not have a completely free hand. Some of his powers are explained on the next page:

The Prime Minister, Tony Blair, prepares to meet the media.

>> Political patronage. This means that the Prime Minister has the right to appoint his supporters to over 100 government positions. These range from the **Chancellor of the Exchequer** to junior government ministers. Having appointed them, he can replace them as he chooses. He also appoints senior civil servants, judges and Church of England bishops.

Limitations: In reality, a Prime Minister has to be very careful about the balance of the Cabinet. Important figures within the party must be appointed to ensure the loyalty of the **MPs**, and different opinions within the party must be represented to ensure loyalty. A geographical, **ethnic** and gender mix is necessary to make sure that the entire country is represented.

>> Foreign policy. The Prime Minister represents Britain at most important meetings with foreign leaders. At European Union summits he or she meets with European heads of government to decide on crucial issues facing the EU. At G8 meetings the Prime Minister meets with the leaders of the world's richest and most powerful nations to help make economic plans on a global scale. In a time of war this role becomes even more important. Ultimately, it would be the Prime Minister who would decide on the use of nuclear weapons.

Limitations: The Prime Minister attends international meetings having already discussed Britain's position with the Cabinet. Treaties with foreign nations must be confirmed by **Parliament**.

>> The dissolution of Parliament. The Prime Minister can decide when to ask the Queen to dissolve a **parliamentary session** and call a **General Election**. This is an important and useful power, as it allows the Prime Minister to decide to call an election when his or her party is popular. Limitations: Under the 1911 Parliament Act, a parliamentary session can last for no more than five years before calling an election. Waiting too long to call an election can be a risky manoeuvre, as the government may become more unpopular.

The Prime Minister's office

In recent years, controversy has grown concerning the role of the Prime Minister's office. This provides the leader with guidance on major national and international issues. Its members tend to be drawn from the PM's political **party** and can hold a great deal of power, although they are not elected members of the government. They are often closer to the PM than members of the Cabinet, but are paid as members of the **civil service**, a body that prides itself in being above party politics. This situation has led to criticism of these 'special advisors', especially from those who fear that Britain is moving towards an American-style 'presidential' form of government.

PARTS OF GOVERNMENT
The Cabinet

The **Cabinet** is at the centre of the British system of **government**. It is normally made up of between eighteen and 26 **ministers** selected by the Prime Minister. Each minister is responsible for a different area of government – for example:

>> Chief Whip – responsible for maintaining party discipline and seeing that MPs support the government when they vote in parliament

>> Home Secretary – concerned with matters such as law and order and immigration

>> **Chancellor of the Exchequer** – oversees the country's finances

>> Foreign Secretary – responsible for foreign policy

>> Secretary of State for Education and Skills – responsible for schools and training.

There are eight other ministers who are always part of the Cabinet, and others who attend meetings when areas under their control are discussed. The ministers accept a 'portfolio,' or an area of government under their control. They must put policy into action in these areas and answer questions from **MPs** in **Parliament** during question time.

The Cabinet usually meets every Thursday in 10 Downing Street, London, the Prime Minister's official residence. There are also smaller Cabinet committees that meet to discuss policy in greater detail. The Cabinet plans new **legislation**, ensures that government departments work together, and discusses any problems that may have arisen. Once a decision has been made in Cabinet, all ministers agree to support it, even any who disagree with it in private. This is known as 'collective responsibility', and is designed to ensure that the government presents a united front at home and abroad.

If a minister thinks that he or she cannot support a decision, then they must resign. This is a powerful weapon for a Cabinet minister, and can be embarrassing for a government. Prime Ministers work hard to make sure all ministers feel able to support government policy. If a minister is not doing the job well, the Prime Minister is responsible for sacking him or her. Again, this is very embarrassing for the Prime Minister. Ministers in this position are normally persuaded to resign.

Question time

Prime Minister's Questions are traditionally an opportunity for the leader of the **opposition** to criticize government policy and to embarrass the Prime Minister. Since Tony Blair became Prime Minister, PM's Questions have been held every Wednesday afternoon when Parliament is sitting. They are broadcast on Radio Five Live and BBC2. The scene is a strange mix of ancient tradition and rowdy behaviour – politics or pantomime: why not watch or listen and decide for yourself?

Who is more powerful – the Prime Minister or the Cabinet?

The Prime Minister chairs Cabinet meetings and some of the more powerful Cabinet committees. In this position, he or she can decide what will be discussed at the meeting – the agenda – and sum up what has been decided at the end. The ministers have all been appointed by the Prime Minister, who is usually their **party** leader, so they will often feel a sense of loyalty to him or her. They also must remember that the Prime Minister can both sack and promote them.

This would seem to make the Prime Minister very powerful, but the Cabinet can put limits on this. Collective responsibility ensures that the Cabinet acts as more than just an official stamp on the Prime Minister's plans. Issues are debated carefully to guarantee a compromise that the whole Cabinet can support: if several ministers were to resign, it would cause great difficulties for the government. Prime Ministers must also be aware that the Cabinet could force them to resign. For example, in 1990 Margaret Thatcher lost the support of her party after an attack by a senior minister, Geoffrey Howe.

The shadow Cabinet

The second largest party in Parliament forms the opposition. The leader of the opposition selects a group of his or her MPs to act as a **Shadow Cabinet**. This mirrors the positions of the government, with a shadow Health Secretary, Chancellor of the Exchequer and so on. The Shadow

Cabinet members argue alternative policies to those of the government, and represent their party in the media. In Parliament, they confront their opponents at each of the government minister's question times. For example, during Prime Minister's question time, the leader of the opposition challenges the Prime Minister and attacks the government.

Prime Minister Blair called an emergency meeting of his Cabinet in March 2003, just before British troops went into action in Iraq.

PARTS OF GOVERNMENT
The Houses of Parliament

The most important principle of the British **constitution** is 'parliamentary sovereignty'. This means that there is no greater power in the land than **Parliament**. Parliament has the power to make or undo laws as it chooses, with no limits placed upon it.

The Houses of Parliament at Westminster are made up of two separate chambers: the House of Lords and the House of Commons. Traditionally the Lords is known as the 'upper house', but in practice it has much less power than the Commons, the 'lower house'. Parliament is often simply called Westminster.

The House of Commons

For the purpose of **General Elections** the United Kingdom is currently divided into 646 **constituencies**. In each of these constituencies, **candidates** from different political **parties** compete with each other to become the **Member of Parliament (MP)** for the area. Once elected, MPs travel to Westminster to take their seats in the House of Commons. Here, they look after the interests of their **constituents**, and debate **government** policy and new legislation.

Frontbenchers and backbenchers

The political party with the greatest number of seats after a General Election forms the government. Around 100 MPs are offered positions in the government. These **ministers** each look after a specific area of policy. The unsuccessful parties also promote some MPs to senior positions. The second largest party takes on the role of official **opposition** and sets up a **Shadow Cabinet**. Other parties also choose spokespersons to shadow government departments. These senior MPs of all parties are known as '**frontbenchers**' because they sit in the front rows of the Commons chamber.

However, most MPs do not receive a frontbench position and so are known as **backbenchers**, sitting behind their party leaders. Although they have not been given a position of power, these MPs still have a very important role to play in making sure that **democracy** is upheld in Parliament.

FIND OUT... 🔍 **>>**

More about how the House of Commons works can be found at www.parliament.uk or you can write to: The Parliamentary Education Unit, Norman Shaw Building (North), London. SW1A 2TT

The Speaker

One MP, known as the Speaker, is expected to be completely neutral in all debates. This officer was originally appointed to Parliament by a royal order, but since the seventeenth century has been the independent chairman of the Commons. The Speaker, who is also an MP but does not always come from the governing party, acts as a kind of referee in debates. He or she calls MPs to speak in turn and see that they stick to the rules of Parliament.

Members of the House of Commons, led by the Speaker Michael Martin (centre) enter the House of Lords for the Queen's Speech.

The House of Lords

The House of Lords is made up of four non-elected groups:

>> Hereditary peers – nobles who have inherited their titles

>> Life peers – lords and ladies whose titles are a reward for service.

>> Church of England bishops

>> Senior judges – known as the Law Lords.

The Lords is currently being reformed and even a name change is planned. Over the last century the Lords has been made more representative of the country as a whole by the introduction of life peers and reducing the power of hereditary peers. This trend will probably continue.

Political parties have less control in the Lords than in the Commons. Indeed, of the 723 lords, 187, known as 'crossbenchers', are independent of any party.

PARTS OF GOVERNMENT
How are laws made?

New **legislation** is introduced in the form of a **bill**. This goes through a long process to become an **Act of Parliament** – the law of the land. Bills are usually proposed by the **government** and are introduced to the House of Commons at their 'first reading'. There is no debate until the 'second reading,' when the bill is debated in the Commons before being passed on to the 'committee stage'. Here, the bill is examined in detail by a specially-formed Standing Committee of MPs, who suggest changes that could be made. These are debated in the Commons at the 'report stage', when other MPs can suggest changes. The bill finishes in the Commons after a final vote known as the 'third reading'. It then goes for discussion in the House of Lords, whose changes, if any, have to be accepted by the Commons. It is not until a final version is agreed by both houses that a bill becomes an Act of Parliament and receives **royal assent**. The diagram on page 19 shows how this process happens.

What does the House of Lords do?

The power of the Lords has declined greatly over the last 100 years. It debates government bills and suggests amendments, or rejects them completely. The House of Commons has the final say, so the Lords can only delay legislation. It also acts as the UK's highest court, with the Law Lords the final court of appeal.

A debate in the House of Lords. Bishops representing the Church of England can be seen on the right.

What powers does an MP have?

>> Control of the government: most of the **Cabinet** is drawn from the House of Commons and is responsible to it. If MPs are unhappy with government legislation, they can change it or vote against it.
Limitations: successful rebellions against **party** leadership are rare. Each party has 'whips' whose job it is to make sure that all MPs are 'whipped into line' and vote the way their party leaders want them to.

>> Question time: the Prime Minister and the Cabinet make themselves available to the Commons for questions.
Limitations: time for questions is limited and MPs must prepare their questions ten days in advance. This gives time for the **civil service** to research the **minister's** answers, making it easier for them to avoid mistakes. MPs try to get around this by following their official question with supplementary questions that the minister must answer without having researched them beforehand.

>> Parliamentary committees: MPs of all parties may be members of Select and Standing committees. Select committees examine the work of the government in a variety of areas, such as health and defence, and their findings can cause problems for governments. Standing committees examine and suggest changes to bills.
Limitations: the party in power normally has a majority on a committee which cannot force ministers to answer their questions.

>> Private Members' bills: MPs are allowed to propose their own bills. Important acts such as those legalizing abortion and homosexuality were introduced as Private Members' bills.
Limitations: MPs are **balloted** and only twenty get the chance to introduce a Private Members' bill during each parliamentary session. The time allowed to debate these bills is limited, so it is rare for them to make it through the legislative progress.

From bill to Act of Parliament

BILL 1	2	3	4
FIRST READING No debate or changes	**SECOND READING** MPs debate the bill as a whole	**COMMITTEE STAGE** Amendments suggested by a Commons committee	**REPORT STAGE** Amendments debated in Commons

5	6	7	ACT 8
THIRD READING MPs vote on the bill	**HOUSE OF LORDS** Peers analyze the bill in detail	**ROYAL ASSENT** Bill becomes law	**Bill becomes ACT OF PARLIAMENT**

PARTS OF GOVERNMENT
Local government

If your local area needs a new bus stop, who do you get in touch with? Should your MP raise the matter in the House of Commons, or would it be the responsibility of the Ministry of Transport? The answer is to ask your local councillor, an elected official who helps to organize public services in your area. Without local **government** it would be impossible to govern the country. Instead of discussing the wider issues that affect our lives, time in the Commons would be taken up discussing bus stops, play areas and rubbish collection.

What does local government do?

The nature and powers of local government in your area will vary depending upon where you live:

>> London: local government in London changed greatly in 2000 when it became the first British city to have a directly elected mayor. The mayor heads the Greater London Authority (GLA), which is responsible for matters such as transport, policing, the fire service, economic development and the environment. The GLA works alongside 33 borough councils that have similar functions to the metropolitan councils elsewhere in the UK (see below).

>> Unitary authorities: also called metropolitan councils, these look after public services in the major cities of England, and in cities and rural areas in Wales. They have wide-ranging powers, including responsibility for education, social services, housing and rubbish collection.

>> Rural areas: these have a three-tier system of local government. At the top are county councils, responsible for policing, the fire service, roads and social services. These are subdivided into district councils that administer housing, town planning, leisure facilities and rubbish collection. On a third level are town and parish councils that control more basic services like footpaths and street lighting.

>> Scotland: here there are 32 unitary authorities with powers similar to those of such authorities south of the border. However, Scottish authorities have to work with an extra tier of government, the **devolved parliament**, which was set up in 1999.

>> Northern Ireland: the province is divided into 26 districts, each with its own elected council. In theory, these have powers similar to English district councils. Unfortunately, the picture in the province is greatly complicated by community 'troubles', which have led to divided councils and many decisions being taken by civil servants rather than by elected representatives of the people.

>>

The future of local government

The introduction of an elected mayor and the GLA in London led to calls for similar arrangements for other English cities. The 2000 Local Government Act provided three options for councils:

>> An elected mayor and a **Cabinet** of councillors appointed by the mayor

>> A leader and a Cabinet of councillors appointed by the leader or the council

>> An elected mayor and a council manager appointed by the council.

The central government hopes that its proposals will make local government more modern, allowing decisions to be made quickly by a team that is clearly identifiable to the people.

Funding and electing local government

Local government employs over two million people in the UK, including teachers, road sweepers, police officers and rubbish collectors. This obviously requires massive funding. Much of this comes from central government at Westminster, but councils also raise their own funding through the council tax. Every adult pays a charge set by the council. The amount varies according to the value of the property in which one lives.

London has an elected Mayor and Cabinet of councillors, appointed by the Mayor. They meet at City Hall on the south bank of the River Thames in London.

Council elections are every four years, with all of the major national **parties** fielding **candidates**. Independent candidates are common and around 50 per cent of rural councillors who get elected are unopposed, so there are plenty of opportunities to get involved in local politics.

Bradford – the challenge to local government

Bradford City Council, a unitary authority, serves a community of around 500,000 people from many ethnic backgrounds. Tragically, in July 2001, the city saw Britain's worst rioting for twenty years. The council's efforts to tackle the causes of the trouble offer a good insight into the way local government works. Here are examples:

>> Education promoting partnerships between schools

>> Employment – attracting new business to the city

>> Safety – establishing city centre wardens

>> Housing – easing access to council housing for minority groups

>> Sport and arts – bidding to become European Capital of Culture

>> Health – co-ordinating the work of local health trusts to ensure equality of care.

More information about Bradford Council can be found at www.bradford.gov.uk.

PARTS OF GOVERNMENT
The influence of Europe

The European Economic Community (EEC) was set up in 1957 to promote trade between member states. It was also intended to develop institutions that would coordinate economic and social policy. Some supporters hoped it would eventually lead to a European government. After much debate, the UK joined the Community in 1974. Since then, Europe has frequently been a source of controversy in British politics. The Maastricht Treaty of 1991 brought the member states closer together in the re-named European Union and paved the way for a single currency, the **Euro**, which several countries adopted in 2002. Even closer union was attempted at Nice in 2003 but plans for a new EU constitution ran into serious opposition.

The institutions of the European Union

>> The Council: this takes the form of meetings of all EU heads of state and, more regularly, a General Council of its Foreign Ministers. Votes in the General Council are allocated according to a state's population. Meetings plan the policies that will put the plans of the European Council into action.

>> The European Commission: Commission members are nominated by the member states, but once in position they are expected to put the EU before their home country's self-interest. It helps to plan the future development of the EU, putting its plans to the Council of Ministers.

>> The European **Parliament**: the 732 Members of the European Parliament (MEPs) are elected from the member states. The number of MEPs each country has depends upon its population; the UK has 78. The Parliament checks legislation, helps draw up the budget, approves appointments to the Commission and generally keeps an eye on the way the EU is run.

>> The European Court of Justice: each member state appoints a judge to the European Court of Justice. Legal decisions taken in any member state can be challenged here, forcing all governments to make sure their domestic laws do not go against those of Europe.

How does the EU affect the UK?

The EU has had a great impact on the way the UK is run. When the British Parliament passed the European Communities Act in 1972, it accepted that laws passed in Europe could override those passed in the UK. Removing trade barriers and tariffs has meant that Europe has become the most important market for British goods. In 1973, only 30 per cent of Britain's exports went to EU member states, but by 2003 this had risen to 54 per cent, making withdrawal from the EU potentially disastrous. The EU has opened up many opportunities for the **citizens** of the UK. Freedom of movement between EU states allow citizens to work anywhere within the EU and travel without the need for **visas**. European funding is also available for a wide range of projects in the poorer areas of the country.

The decision to incorporate the European Convention on **Human Rights** into British law allows British citizens to challenge the government in British courts – previously, they had to travel to the European Court of Justice.

The European debate

Since the UK joined the European Community in 1974, the organization's powers have grown greatly. Many people in British politics believe EU leaders want to create a 'United States of Europe' that will undermine national governments. Their opponents believe a more united Europe will lead to improved prosperity for the people of the continent. The problem is well illustrated by the debate over the Euro, the European currency, in use since 2002:

>> For many, swapping the pound sterling for the Euro would be a step too far. They say British politicians would lose control over the country's economy. This might cause hardship, as economic policies that suit one part of Europe would not necessarily suit the UK.

>> Supporters of the Euro argue that Britain's industries would benefit from adopting the Euro. They could be sure of the **exchange rate**, allowing better planning and improving their competitiveness.

>> A third group believe Britain should wait to see how the Euro settles down in other countries before adopting it as the currency in Britain.

DEMOCRACY IN ACTION
What is democracy?

In ancient Greece, the **citizens** of a city-state would meet regularly to decide on how their state would be run. This system was known as *demokratia*, from demos (people) and kratos (rule). This would be impossible in modern Britain; 59 million people cannot meet and make decisions! In our **democracy**, we elect representatives to make decisions on our behalf – the **Members of Parliament**. Our **General Elections** must be held at least every five years.

The campaign trail

When the Prime Minister decides it is time to call a **General Election**, he or she asks the **monarch** to dissolve **Parliament**, allowing the election campaigns to begin. Each political **party** produces a national **manifesto**, a document that sets out its plans for **government**, and summaries of this are delivered to the homes of everyone who can vote. Local **candidates** also produce pamphlets that outline what they feel they can offer a **constituency**. Posters urging voters to support different candidates appear in windows and on lamp posts as parties do their best to promote their cause. On a national level, the leader and senior figures often board 'battle

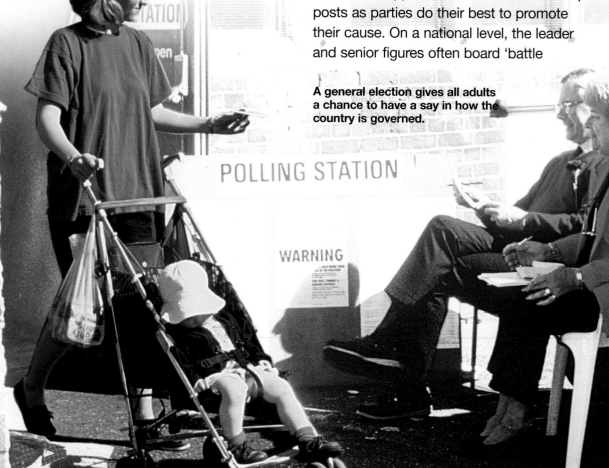

A general election gives all adults a chance to have a say in how the country is governed.

POLLING STATION

WARNING

General Election result, June 2005

PARTY	NUMBER OF VOTES	PERCENTAGE OF VOTES	NUMBER OF SEATS	PERCENTAGE OF SEATS
LABOUR	9,562,122	35.3	356	55.2
CONSERVATIVES	8,772,598	32.3	198	30.7
LIBDEMS	5,981,874	22.1	62	9.6
OTHERS*	2,663,816	10.3	30	4.5

* Northern Irish parties, Scottish and Welsh Nationalists and Independents

buses' to tour the country drumming up support. Their visits often focus on marginal constituencies – places that saw a tight result in the previous election and could be won or lost. The media plays an important role in these campaigns. Newspaper advertisements are placed and all parties with more than 100 candidates are entitled to produce party political broadcasts. These are short TV and radio presentations that allow a political party to put forward their plans.

How do we elect our representatives?

The campaign continues right up to Election Day, when the people of the country reveal which party has impressed them most. The UK is divided into 659 constituencies, each electing one Member of Parliament. These constituencies can vary greatly in size, but all contain around the same number of people, ensuring that every citizen has an equal representation in Parliament. The MPs are elected under the 'first-past-the-post' system. This means that on Election Day, each voter selects the candidate they prefer and puts an 'X'

beside that candidate's name on a slip of paper. The candidate with the greatest number of votes wins. The party with the most MPs forms the government, and its leader becomes Prime Minister.

Other voting systems

First-past-the-post is not the only voting system used in the UK. In elections for the European Parliament, a system of **proportional representation (PR)** is used. Instead of 646 small constituencies, the country is divided into twelve large regional constituencies. Voters place candidates in order of preference, and between three and ten members are returned for each region, giving 78 MEPs in total. A similar system is used in elections for the Northern Ireland Assembly. The Scottish Parliament and Welsh Assembly are elected under another version of PR, called the Additional Member System. Each **elector** has two votes, one for the candidate of his or her choice, the second for a political party. These second votes are then used to elect additional members, chosen from party lists. This system is designed to ensure that each party gets a share of seats in proportion to the number of votes it receives.

DEMOCRACY IN ACTION
What are political parties?

All **democratic** countries have political **parties**. These are groups of people who broadly agree how they think the country should be run. Together, they try to get their party members elected into government, so that they can put their ideas into action.

Political parties in Britain

Towards the end of the seventeenth century, two political groupings emerged in the English **Parliament** – the Whigs and the Tories (see pages 8–9). These were very different from modern political parties. They had no central organization and were really just loose gatherings of **MPs** who voted together in the Commons and Lords.

This changed as the Reform Acts of the nineteenth century (see pages 8–9) extended the franchise (the right to vote). Many more voters required new, sophisticated ways of getting in touch with them. The parties responded by setting up central offices to plan electoral campaigns and attract supporters. **Constituency** party branches were added to organize campaigns locally. By 1914, Britain had the party system that we know today, with the Conservative, Liberal and Labour parties competing for the people's votes.

www.libdems.org.uk

Former Leader of the LibDem party, Charles Kennedy, speaking at the annual party conference.

>>

What do political parties do?

Political parties play a very important role in any democracy. Without them Parliament would just be a gatherings of MPs, all with different aims. This would make **government** impossible. Parties are organized on national and **constituency** levels, with the latter giving local members the opportunity to influence the leadership and its policies. Here are some of the things that political parties do:

>> Elections: the national and constituency parties select the **candidates** for **General Elections**. Most party central offices produce approved candidate lists, and each constituency party selects its prospective MP. Having done this, the constituency membership is expected to campaign locally on behalf of their candidate. Meanwhile, party central offices organize the national campaign through party political broadcasts, a party **manifesto**, TV and radio interviews and so on.

>> Organizing Parliament and providing the government: once the House of Commons is elected, parties enable it to function efficiently. This is done by arranging the complicated timetable of legislation and votes. Even before that, the majority party has formed the government that runs the country.

>> Making policy: ideas for new legislation come from a wide range of sources: pressure groups, institutions such as universities, the media and even groups chatting in the pub. It is the task of parties to sift through the mass of suggestions, seeing which are popular and feasible, and turning these into workable laws.

Should political parties be funded by the state?

Political party funding has been an area of controversy in recent years. Critics have argued that relying on donations from individuals and companies leads to parties being under pressure to favour the needs of these donors. This problem was demonstrated in November 1997, when the Labour Prime Minister Tony Blair announced that Formula 1 motor racing would not face a ban on tobacco sponsorship in sport. It was claimed that the decision was made because a ban might force the sport to move to Eastern Europe, taking with it thousands of jobs. However, critics pointed out that the Labour Party had just received a donation of £1 million from the head of Formula 1, Bernie Ecclestone.

Had the Prime Minister been influenced by the donation? Both Ecclestone and Blair denied this was the case, but it led to demands for Britain to follow the example of other European countries and introduce state funding of political parties.

DEMOCRACY IN ACTION
Britain's political parties

Three major political **parties** dominate the British political system. Although their policies change at every election, they each claim to represent the interests of the British people.

The Conservative Party

The Conservative Party emerged from the Tory Party of the seventeenth and eighteenth centuries, changing its name in the mid-nineteenth century. The name 'Conservative' is derived from the party's tradition of trying to conserve the ancient institutions of the UK – the monarchy, House of Lords, unwritten **constitution** and the unions with Scotland and Northern Ireland. The party is traditionally opposed to **radical** change, arguing that evolution, not revolution, has brought the UK prosperity.

The party is organized on three levels. Conservative Central Office is responsible for the administration of the party, while the Parliamentary Party of Conservative **MPs** makes up its representation in the Commons. The National Union of Conservative Associations represents **constituency** branches. Reforms of the late twentieth century gave ordinary members greater influence within the party. However, electoral failure and the selection of a string of unsuccessful party leaders has led to calls for power to be restored to Conservative MPs.

The Liberal Democrats

The Liberal Democrat party has its origins in the Whigs, who became the Liberal Party in the mid-nineteenth century. Traditionally promoting the rights of the individual, the original Liberals supported the middle class and business, and gradually began to press for social reform to allow the working class greater freedom. Along with the Conservatives, they dominated British politics until the First World War, when the Labour Party began to attract their working class supporters. In 1981, they joined with the Social Democrats to create the Alliance. The two merged in 1987. The LibDems now regard themselves as the party that best represents the middle ground in British politics, although their policies are often more radical than either Labour or the Conservatives. Party members have great influence within the organization, and the party conference is the supreme policy-making body.

FIND OUT...

For more information on how to join the different main political parties, go to: www.labour.org.uk
www.conservatives.com
www.libdems.org.uk

The Labour Party

The Labour Party grew out of the **trade union** movement of the early twentieth century. It aimed to give the working class a voice in **Parliament**. Quickly overtaking the Liberal Party, it has competed for power with the Conservatives since the First World War. Its policies fell out of favour with voters in the late 1970s, leading to a move towards the centre in the 1990s. This led to the election of Tony Blair's 'New Labour' government in 1997. Blair's reforms took power away from the trade unions and increased the influence of constituency parties. Representatives from constituency parties can now influence policy through the National Policy Forum. They also have representatives on the party's governing body, the National Executive. The election of the party leadership also changed, with each member having an equal vote.

Britain has many smaller parties representing different interests. Some are regional, such as the Scottish National Party, which sends MPs to Westminster but also has influence in the Scottish Parliament. Other parties represent certain issues. The Green Party, for instance, campaigns on environmental issues.

Party policy

The table below shows the policies of the three main political parties.

Party policy in the 2005 General Election

ISSUE	LABOUR (Leader: Tony Blair)	LIBDEMS (Leader: Charles Kennedy)	CONSERVATIVE (Present Leader: David Cameron)
TAXATION AND ECONOMIC POLICY	No tax increases, maintain strong economy and low inflation.	Local income tax to replace Council Tax. Raise income tax on the very wealthy.	£4 billion tax cuts.
EUROPE	Back EU constitution. Join Europe when suitable.	Strongly support EU constitution and membership of the Euro.	Oppose EU constitution. Reject Euro.
EDUCATION	More specialist schools. Top-up university fees and grants for the poorest.	Cut class sizes and 'unnecessary' tests. Scrap tuition fees.	Boost choice. More school places. No student fees.
HEALTH	Patient choice. Cut waiting times. 100 new hospitals.	Free long-term care. Dental and eye tests.	Scrap many targets. Financial help to go private. More power to matrons.
LAW AND ORDER AND IMMIGRATION	Community support officers. More prison places. Tougher rules on immigration.	10,000 more police officers. Plans to stop re-offending. Decriminalise cannabis.	Immigration quotas. 40,000 more police officers. 20,000 more prison places.
WAR ON TERROR AND WAR IN IRAQ	Pursue war in Iraq. Greater powers against terror suspects.	Oppose Iraq war. Judges only to detain terror suspects.	Maintain Iraq war. Increase defence and anti-terror spending.

DEMOCRACY IN ACTION
Pressure groups

The role of all the levels of **government** in the UK is to decide upon and put into practice policies that cover a wide range of issues. However, for many **citizens** one policy causes them most concern. These individuals often join pressure groups, which are organizations that hope to influence government policy in a specific area or to promote a certain cause. Pressure groups represent a wide variety of interests and have varying degrees of influence, but all provide an important opportunity for citizens to make their views and opinions heard. They aim to ensure that the government hears, and listens to, the views of their members.

Different types of pressure groups

There are thousands of pressure groups in the UK ranging from community organizations which put pressure on their local councils, to **trade unions** trying to influence industry and the government. The majority, however, fall into three main categories:

>> Sectional groups: these represent a particular section of society, doing their best to protect their members' interests and put forward their views. Some have a lot of influence. Trade unions are capable of putting a great deal of pressure on governments on behalf of their members, while the views of the employers' body, the Confederation of British Industries (CBI), are rarely ignored. Other sectional groups rarely make the news, only coming into the public eye when their members' interests are threatened.

>> Promotional groups: perhaps the most familiar type of pressure group, these organizations are interested in promoting a particular political or moral cause, rather than the interests of their members. They include the Royal Society for the Prevention of Cruelty to Animals (RSPCA), the Campaign for Nuclear Disarmament (CND) and the Friends of the Earth.

>> 'Fire brigade' groups: as their name suggests, these groups emerge to argue against a particular proposal, then quickly disappear, often enlisting the support of other, permanent organizations. Residents' groups are often formed to fight schemes such as new roads, power stations and mobile phone masts, trying to protect their community and way of life. Others are formed to campaign on behalf of hospitals and schools threatened with closure.

What tactics do pressure groups use?

Major changes in public services, such as health and education, are unlikely to go ahead without consultation with the unions involved, such as the National Union of Teachers, or the British Medical Association, which represents doctors. This gives those they represent a great deal of influence by embarrassing the government through **strike** action and media publicity.

The less influential promotional and fire brigade groups cannot call strike action to promote their cause, and few are able to influence the government directly. They use a variety of tactics to promote their causes.

Protest and counter-protest – the fox hunting debate

Fox hunting has long been a controversial issue in British society, and a prolonged campaign against it finally met with success in January 2001, when the Commons passed a **bill** banning the sport. The League Against Cruel Sports, which had been at the forefront of the campaign, hailed the new bill as a victory. The group had organized demonstrations at fox hunts across the country, organized letter-writing campaigns and taken out newspaper advertisements to keep the issue in the public eye.

The introduction of the bill had led to the formation of a pro-hunting pressure group, the Countryside Alliance, which brought thousands of people to London in huge protest marches. They gained a short-term victory, when the House of Lords rejected the Commons bill. This delayed the passing of the legislation until November 2004.

More about the views and tactics of the two groups can be found at: www.league.uk.com and www.countryside-alliance.org.uk

Mass marches were central to the Countryside Alliance's campaign to protect fox hunting.

DEMOCRACY IN ACTION
Pressure groups at work

Greenpeace campaigners often use the media to try to embarrass companies into acting to protect the environment.

The environment

Many pressure groups deal with issues that cross national boundaries. Greenpeace and Friends of the Earth have built up huge international memberships in their attempts to promote environmental concerns. Recently, they have campaigned for full international agreement on protecting the environment. In particular, they want universal support for the Kyoto Treaty. This is an international agreement that aims to limit the effects of greenhouse gases on the environment. Both groups have also been involved with campaigns that may otherwise have been regarded as local protests, such as the protests against the environmental impact of new roads.

Human rights

This is another area in which pressure groups operate worldwide. In many countries it is difficult, sometimes impossible, for people to come together to protest, and those who do often find themselves imprisoned. Amnesty International was formed in 1961 to campaign on behalf of such **political prisoners**, or prisoners of conscience, around the world. They have held public demonstrations and fundraising concerts, as well as becoming involved in **human rights** education in schools. They are perhaps most famous for organizing mass

>>

letter-writing campaigns in support of political prisoners. Letters demanding their release are sent to embassies and **government** officials, making them aware that their treatment of the prisoners is being closely watched. Such letters have made an impact – one former torturer from El Salvador has said '...if there's lots of pressure – like from Amnesty International or some foreign countries – we might pass them on to a judge. But if there's no pressure, then they're dead.' Amnesty's successes clearly show how an individual can make a difference, even to a global cause.

'Fire brigade' groups

When Britain invaded Iraq alongside the US in March 2003, the action was strongly opposed by the Stop the War Coalition. This single-issue pressure group drew hundreds of thousands to its meetings but failed to force the government to alter its policy. Indeed, pressure groups do not need mass membership to influence national polictics. In autumn 2000, for instance, a group of farmers and lorry drivers brought Britain to a halt and forced the government to change its policy on fuel taxes. Angered by rising fuel prices, the protestors caused great inconvenience and attracted widespread popular support by blocking key routes. Although unsuccessful in their aim of reducing fuel prices immediately, the following year's budget reversed previous policy of annual fuel tax rises.

Using the democratic process

UK elections are dominated by the major **parties**, but often **candidates** stand to publicize a particular cause. The Green Party, which campaigns on environmental issues, has had limited success in elections, gaining several council seats and good support in European elections. At **General Elections** however, the national political parties tend to squeeze out the pressure group parties. A recent exception occurred in the 2005 election when the ex-labour MP George Galloway formed the Respect Party to challenge the Labour government's war in Iraq. Remarkably, Galloway overturned a 10,500 Labour majority (2001) to win the Bethnal Green and Bow constituency. Respect also pushed the Conservatives into third place in East Ham and West Ham.

FIND OUT...

What are the issues that you feel strongly about? Are you worried about the effect we are having on our environment? Do you want to speak out against cruelty towards animals? There is probably a pressure group that can help you find out more about the issue and represent your views.

You can find out more about the pressure groups discussed here by looking at their web sites.

Try the following:
www.foeeurope.org
www.greenpeace.org.uk
www.amnesty.org
www.respectcoalition.org
www.healthconcern.org.uk
www.greenparty.org.uk
www.scottishgreens.org.uk

REGIONAL VARIATIONS
Wales

Devolution

The Acts of Union of 1707 and 1801 meant that all parts of the UK were governed directly from Westminster. Scottish, Welsh and Irish **politicians** had to travel to London to add their voices to the debates in **Parliament**. Recently this changed. **Devolution** has meant that separate assemblies have been created for the 'Celtic nations'. Some power has been transferred away from Westminster, and local politicians have begun to make decisions for their people. How did this come about?

Wales was ruled from London for nearly 800 years, but always maintained a clear national identity. Many people, including the Welsh **Nationalist Party**, Plaid Cymru, argued that the Westminster Parliament was dominated by English MPs who could not look after the interests of the Welsh. As a result, they said, Welsh culture and language suffered, and decisions were being made to suit English, not Welsh, needs. In 1997, the new Labour **government** accepted these arguments, and put forward plans to devolve powers to Wales. In September 1997, the Welsh people narrowly supported the proposals in a **referendum**, with 50.3 per cent voting in favour of a separate Welsh parliament. The way was open for the creation of a new 60-seat National Assembly.

Welsh Nationalism has often been focused on the International Rugby team.

How is the Assembly elected?

The first two elections were held in May 1999 and May 2003. The election process is different from UK **General Elections**. Each member of the **electorate** has two votes. The first is used to select a **constituency** member in the same way as Westminster elections, and 40 members are elected in this way. The second vote goes into one of five regional counts under the Additional Member System, a form of **proportional representation**. The top four **candidates** are elected from each region.

The first National Assembly met to elect its First **Minister** on 12 May 1999. He then selected his Assembly **cabinet**, with ministers responsible for many of the things that Westminster had previously controlled. These powers had come into force on 1 July 1999.

What powers does the Welsh Assembly have?

The 1998 Government of Wales Act devolved several powers to the new Assembly; others were kept by Westminster. The Assembly is responsible for a wide range of domestic affairs, but only those that affect Wales. Westminster has kept control of primary **legislation** – for example, it might say that all schools should follow a national curriculum. The Assembly controls how that plan is put into action – through secondary legislation, it would be able to decide what subjects this curriculum would have in Wales. Importantly, the Welsh Assembly receives a **Budget** to spend on its domestic services as it chooses, but it cannot raise or lower taxes. Some of the areas the Assembly is responsible for are:

>> Agriculture and the environment

>> Economic development and transport

>> Health and the health service

>> Education, culture and the Welsh language

>> Housing and town planning.

These powers allow members of the Welsh Assembly to make important decisions that affect the Welsh people. They direct funding for hospitals and schools, work to attract and support business and balance the needs of industry with those of the environment.

Plaid Cymru

Plaid Cymru was set up in 1925 to campaign for Welsh independence. It first attracted support in rural, Welsh-speaking areas, but seemed doomed to failure when a vote in 1979 rejected devolution. The long period of Conservative government between 1979 and 1997 revived its fortunes. Wales was a traditional Labour stronghold, and its people felt increasingly isolated from a mainly English administration. Support for both Plaid Cymru and devolution grew, with the party winning four seats in the 1997 General Election. The party was disappointed by the 1997 referendum. It went on to capture seventeen of the 60 seats in 1997, but only twelve in 2003.

FIND OUT...

Find out more about the Welsh political parties and their attitudes to devolution:

The National Assembly:
www.wales.gov.uk

Plaid Cymru:
www.plaidcymru.org

The Welsh Labour Party:
www.welshlabour.org.uk

The Welsh Conservative Party:
www.welsh-conservatives.org.uk

The Welsh Liberal Democrats:
www.welshlibdems.org.uk

REGIONAL VARIATIONS
Scotland

Although the Act of Union in 1707 brought England and Scotland together under one **Parliament**, the terms of the act allowed Scotland to retain many of its old institutions, such as its legal and educational systems. This has helped to preserve Scotland's national identity and helped to encourage a desire for independence, with the Scottish National **Party** as the focus of these desires.

As in Wales, a **referendum** on **devolution** was held in Scotland in 1997, with a majority in favour – 74 per cent of the population supported the plan.

Electing the Scottish Parliament

Using an electoral system that mirrors that of Wales, on 6 May 1999 the Scots elected their first Parliament for almost 300 years. 129 members of the Scottish Parliament (MSP) were elected. Each elector cast two votes, one for the 73 MSPs representing local **constituencies**, the other to help choose 56 members from regional lists. In 1999 and again in 2003, Labour emerged as the largest party, although with no overall majority. The table below shows how proportional representation works. Without it, for example, the Scottish National Party would have polled 22 per cent of the vote but won only nine (seven per cent) of the seats.

Representation of the major parties in the Scottish parliament, 2003

PARTY	CONSTITUENCY	LIST	TOTAL	% OF VOTES*	% OF SEATS*
CONSERVATIVE	3	15	18	16	14
LABOUR	46	4	50	32	39
LIBERAL DEMOCRATS	13	4	17	13.5	13
SNP	9	18	27	22	21
OTHERS	2	15	17	16.5	13

* Average of constituency and list ballots

Source: Scottish parliament website

Shortly after each election the Labour leader was chosen as Scotland's First Minister and a coalition administration was formed between Labour and the Liberal Democrats.

What powers does the Scottish parliament have?

The Scottish Parliament has wider ranging powers than the assemblies in Wales and Northern Ireland. Importantly, it has the right to raise or lower income tax by up to three pence, and it also receives a **budget** from Westminster. This allows it some freedom to develop policies and put them into action. Already the Parliament has been able to remove university fees for Scottish students, and provide a pay increase for teachers that is greater than in the rest of the UK. The Parliament also controls law and order, the police and the judiciary (courts), reflecting the independent traditions and procedure of Scottish law.

A debate in the Scottish Parliament. Great efforts have been made to make its proceedings as open and accessible to the public as possible.

The Scottish National Party

The Scottish National Party (SNP) was set up in 1934 to campaign for independence. It was at its most powerful in the 1970s, with eleven **MPs** returned in the 1974 election. As with Plaid Cymru in Wales, the failure of the 1979 referendum on devolution was a set back. However, the SNP's fortunes revived while the Conservatives were in office, 1979–1997. Its members were divided over devolution as an acceptable alternative to independence before agreeing that the Scottish Parliament offers Scotland's best opportunity for self-rule. Although the Scottish National Party lost seats in 2003, its drive for independence was also supported by incoming Green and Socialist MSPs.

FIND OUT...

Find out more about the Scottish Parliament and the political parties represented in it by looking at the following web sites:

The Scottish Parliament:
www.scottish.parl.uk

The Scottish Labour Party:
www.scottishlabour.org

The Scottish National Party:
www.snp.org

The Scottish Conservative and Unionist Party:
www.scottishtories.org

The Scottish Liberal Democrats:
www.scotlibdems.org.uk

REGIONAL VARIATIONS
Northern Ireland

In 1801, an Irish Parliament agreed to Ireland becoming part of the United Kingdom. This minority decision raised strong opposition and, in 1922, after bitter fighting, 26 of the island's largely Catholic counties formed the Irish Free State (Eire). Northern Ireland remained in the UK with its own **parliament** at Stormont.

The Troubles

Northern Ireland has a **Protestant** majority, called **Unionists**, who want to be part of the UK. There is also a substantial **Catholic** minority, many of whom (the **Nationalists** or Republicans) want a united Ireland. During the fifty years of Stormont rule, the Unionist majority always controlled the parliament. The Nationalists felt isolated and discriminated against. In 1969, street violence flared and **Republican** and **Loyalist** terrorist groups soon emerged.

The British Army was called in to maintain law and order, and in 1972 the Westminster **government** suspended the Stormont parliament and took over the government of Northern Ireland. The violence continued for the next 25 years, leaving 3,500 dead and thousands more injured.

The Good Friday Agreement

In 1995, the main terrorist groups on both sides declared a ceasefire so that political talks could begin. Three years of negotiations followed before a breakthrough came on Good Friday 1998. For the first time Unionists and Republicans agreed on a way forward for Northern Ireland. A **referendum** on both sides of the Irish border followed, showing overwhelming support for the deal.

The years of religious conflict that destroyed the political process in Northern Ireland have made it extremely difficult for true democracy to re-emerge.

The agreement set up a 108-member power sharing assembly with ten ministerial departments. After an election in May 1998, David Trimble of the Ulster Unionist **Party** (UUP) was selected as First **Minister**, with Seamus Mallon of the Nationalist SDLP as his deputy. Other posts were allocated to the most successful parties. The UUP and SDLP had three ministers; the DUP and Sinn Fein both had two.

What powers does the Assembly have?

The Northern Ireland Assembly has similar powers to that of the assembly in Wales. However, it differs from Scotland and Wales in the way it passes laws. In Northern Ireland a majority of both Unionists and Nationalists must agree on a piece of legislation for it to become law. This prevents domination by one group. A balanced cabinet is responsible for areas such as an economic development, health, agriculture and education.

An uncertain future

In October 2002, the Northern Ireland Assembly was suspended and Westminster once again took over the government of the troubled province. Devolved administration had broken down because of lack of trust between the Republicans and Unionists. Two issues in particular divided them: the refusal of some Nationalist groups to give up their weapons and links between ex-paramilitaries and organized crime.

Who's who in Northern Ireland

PARTY	No. of seats at Westminster 2005
ULSTER UNIONIST PARTY	
Once the largest policital party in Northern Ireland, since the Good Friday Agreement the UUP has lost support to the uncompromising DUP (see bleow). The Agreement paved the way for the UUP's David Trimble to become Northern Ireland's First Minister.	1
DEMOCRATIC UNIONIST PARTY	
Led by the staunchly Protestant Rev. Ian Paisley, the DUP has been the focus of those protestants unwilling to come to terms with the Catholic Nationalists, whom they accuse of being terrorists.	9
SOCIAL DEMOCRATIC AND LABOUR PARTY	
Established in 1970, the Nationalist SDLP works for the unification of Ireland through peaceful means. Its leader, John Hume, worked tirelessly to bring about the Good Friday Agreement.	3
SINN FEIN	
Led by Gerry Adams, Sinn Fein is the political wing of the irish Republican Army (IRA) that sought to unite Ireland by force. Under pressure from London and Dublin, Sinn Fein gradually disassociated itself from extreme violence and accepted the Good Friday Agreement.	5

*There are several other smaller Unionist parties with eight seats, all of which are opposed to the agreement.

PART 6

DEBATE
Look to the future – issues for discussion

The British **constitution** is unwritten, allowing our system of government constantly to evolve. This happens through new laws, conventions and practices, and sometimes through decisions made by judges and politicians of the EU. The following four pages look at some of the issues currently in the news which might well lead to constitutional change over the next few years.

The crowds and media gather outside the Houses of Parliament. The media have an important role to play in informing us about these issues.

Should the UK have a written constitution?

Most countries have a written constitution, and for many years there has been a debate about whether Britain should have one too. A written constitution might set strict rules about the powers of each branch of government. Such rules are called checks and balances. For example, in the USA, new laws require the approval and support of both the President (the Executive) and Congress (the Legislature). Even then, the judiciary (the courts) can declare the new law unconstitutional. In Britain, the Executive (the Prime Minister and **Cabinet**) is controlled by **Parliament**, but since the Executive has a **party** majority in the Commons, this control is rarely exercised. So long as there is a parliamentary majority for a piece of **legislation** there is nothing to stop it becoming law.

For a written constitution: reformers are concerned that Parliament can make and change laws as it sees fit. They argue that there should be checks and balances in government to make sure that no branch has too much power. If Britain had a written constitution, **citizens** would be able to challenge new laws in the courts. Then judges would rule whether a law was within the bounds of the constitution or not.

Against a written constitution: those opposed to a US-style system of checks and balances argue that unelected judges should play no part in the legislative process. Some feel that judges are unrepresentative of the people – they are mainly white males, so could be biased in their interpretation of the constitution. It is also argued that our unwritten constitution has served the country well and arguments over the wording of a constitution would cause division and uncertainty. Moreover, a constitution written today would reflect our values and therefore restrict future generations. After the London Bombings of July 2005, for instance, it was argued that a written constitution might have restricted the government's ability to bring in emergency anti-terrorist legislation.

Why do we still have a monarchy?

Like the constitution, the position of the monarchy has evolved over hundreds of years. Most of its role is now ceremonial, but nevertheless, constitutionally the **monarch** remains **head of state**.

Against a monarchy: for many it is time to find a replacement. They argue that the monarchy is outdated and expensive, and the fact that a royal title is inherited through birth is out of step with the modern world, in which people should gain recognition because of their abilities. Instead of uniting the people, it acts as a symbol of class divisions. Those who support this view feel that it is time Britain became a **republic**, with an elected head of state.

For a monarchy: supporters of the monarchy argue that an unelected monarch is baove party politics, providing a figurehead that everyone can look to in times of national crisis. The monarchy probably costs less then a president would and much of the money is recovered through tourism and other commercial benefits. Windsor Castle and Buckingham Palce, for example, are extremely popular tourist attractions. Finally, the role of an elected president might clash with that of the Prime Minister.

What will happen to the House of Lords?

The House of Lords has changed greatly in the last few years, with a huge reduction in the number of **hereditary peers**. At the moment, their replacements are life peers, nominated by the government and party leaders. For some reformers, these changes have not been enough. Some argue that the Lords remains undemocratic and that it should be replaced by an elected second chamber. This would allow some power to be transferred from the Commons. Opponents fear that this could lead to deadlock between the two houses. Others argue that the Lords should be abolished completely, leaving only the Commons as the elected voice of the people. However, this proposal would put an immense workload on the Commons, and remove an essential counter-balance to the power of the government.

DEBATE
More issues for discussion

What electoral system should we have?

Britain's 'first-past-the-post' electoral system often produces results that favour the two main **parties**: Labour and Conservatives. The number of seats the parties gain does not accurately reflect the number of votes they receive, with smaller parties losing out. The Liberal Democrats have often been the biggest losers under the system, as they often come second in a large number of constituencies. The result of the 1987 **General Election** illustrates the drawbacks of the system.

1987 General Election result

PARTY	VOTES (MILLIONS)	SEATS	PERCENTAGE OF VOTES	PERCENTAGE OF SEATS
CONSERVATIVE	13.7	376	42.2	57.8
LABOUR	10.0	229	30.8	35.2
LIBERAL-SDP	7.3	22	22.6	3.4
OTHERS	1.4	23	4.4	3.5

For Welsh Nationalists, devolution is regarded as a first step towards an independent state. Will devolution break up the United Kingdom?

Not surprisingly, the Liberal Democrats are strong supporters of electoral reform, arguing for a system of **proportional representation** (PR). Two systems of PR are suggested for Britain, the Single Transferable Vote and the Additional Member system. These are already in use in the UK's devolved assemblies (see pages 34–39). Using PR, the Liberal Democrats would have gained around 150 seats in 1987 rather than 22. Opponents of PR say it would lead to weak **coalition governments** because no single party would have an outright majority, making it difficult to introduce **legislation**. Others feel that the multi-member **constituencies** and party lists required by PR would take away the connection between the **constituent** and the **MP**, perhaps reducing the opportunity for local issues to be raised in **Parliament**.

What changes will devolution bring?

The late 1990s saw the transfer of power from Westminster to new devolved assemblies in Scotland, Wales and Northern Ireland. This raised several questions, most importantly what role MPs from the UK's 'Celtic fringe' should have in Parliament, and whether the regions of England should also have their own assemblies. It has been argued that since devolution, MPs from Scotland, the most powerful of the assemblies, should be barred from voting in Westminster on matters that come under the power of the Scottish Parliament. For example, as Scotland's education is administered from Edinburgh, MSPs would be unable to influence education in the rest of the UK. It is also claimed that as Scotland is currently over-represented at Westminster, it should have its representation there cut to just 39 seats. This would reduce the power of the Labour Party, which has strong support in Scotland.

Some have argued that devolution has left the regions of England under-represented. Voters in Scotland, Wales and Northern Ireland can have their grievances looked at by their assembly members and by their Westminster MPs. English voters have no such double representation. Interestingly, they do not appear to want it either. Labour proposals for regional assemblies in England stirred little enthusiasm and in 2005 voters in the north-east rejected a planned assembly in their region.

FURTHER RESOURCES

This book includes many ideas for research through the websites of government and other organizations. These pages list some other sources of information that you may find useful in finding out more about government and citizenship.

Useful addresses

The Hansard Society

St Philips Building,
London School of Economics,
Sheffield Street,
London WC2 2EX.

Tel: 020 7955 7459

Website: www.hansardsociety.org.uk.

This society focuses on increasing people's knowledge about Parliament and government. It can also provide materials to help you stage mock elections in your school.

Citizenship Foundation

15 St Swithins Lane,
London EC4N 8AL.

Tel: 020 7929 3344

Website: www.citfou.org.uk.

An organization dedicated to developing knowledge of the rights and duties of citizenship. Initiatives include the Youth Parliament.

Parliamentary Education Unit

Norman Shaw Building (North),
London SW1A 2TT.

Tel: 020 7219 2105

Website: www.explore.parliament.uk.

The Parliamentary Education Unit is the place to go for information about the Houses of Parliament and the government. The Explore Parliament website has many features including an online debating chamber.

Charter 88

18A Victoria Park Square,
London E2 9PB.

Website: www.charter88.org.uk.

Charter 88 is a pressure group that campaigns for reform in the UK's government organizations.

Further reading

UK Government and Politics in Context
by David Simpson

Culture and Identity
by David Abbott

The Prime Minister and Cabinet Government
by Neil McNaughton

All above are parts of the *Access to Politics* series published by Hodder and Stoughton.

Citizenship by Philip Steele, Evans, 2005

It would be a great help in studying this area to regularly read a daily or Sunday newspaper. In addition you can find in-depth news coverage on Newsnight on BBC 2 and Channel 4 News.

Websites

Excellent background to political issues as well as an easily accessible guide to the British Political system can be found on the BBC News Website at:
www.news.bbc.co.uk.

Another useful site providing information on all aspects of the UK government is:
www.direct.gov.uk

An accessible website offering an introduction to government services and information based on where you live in the UK can be found at:
www.ukonline.gov.uk

A good overview of the political and current affairs situation, with regular updates, news features and items about the Prime Minister, can be found at the Number 10 Downing Street website:
www.number-10.gov.uk

You can read all about the Houses of Parliament, what the two houses each do and what is currently passing through Parliament at:
www.parliament.uk

Find out the latest financial news and information about the Budget at the website of Her Majesty's Treasury:
www.hm-treasury.gov.uk

For a more traditional view of our government, visit the website of the monarchy at: **www.royal.gov.uk**.

You will be also able to find out how to contact your MP or the local council council in your local area. The council will probably have a website describing local services and detailing how they spend their budgets.

GLOSSARY

Act of Parliament	a law passed by both Houses of Parliament
asylum	protection from danger, the term is used particularly about those who leave their country to seek asylum because of persecution for their religious or political beliefs
backbencher	an MP who is not a senior spokesman of either the government or the opposition
ballot	a vote
Bill	a government proposal to change the law. If passed by Parliament, it becomes an Act of Parliament
Budget	the government's plans for how it will raise money for running the country
Cabinet	the senior ministers who meet to plan government policy
candidate	someone who puts themselves forward for election
Catholic	a member of the Roman Catholic Church
Chancellor of the Excheque	the government minister responsible for the country's finances
citizen	a member of a country
civil service	the service responsible for administering the government's plans
Civil War	the English Civil War was fought between the supporters of the King and those of Parliament
coalition	an alliance between political parties to form a government
Commonwealth	a group of countries which used to be part of the British Empire and still retain some links with the UK
constituency	a district which elects a Member of Parliament. The UK is divided into 646 constituencies.
constituent	anyone living in a constituency
constitution	the set of rules under which a country is governed
democracy	a government by representatives elected by the people
devolve, devolution	passing power from the Westminster Parliament to regional assemblies, for instance the Welsh or Scottish Assembly
dictator	a ruler who holds all of the power
electorate	people entitled to vote
ethnic	relating to a particular culture or race
Euro	the shared currency of the European Union
exchange rate	the rate at which the currency of one country can be exchanged for another
frontbencher	a senior spokesman of either the government or the opposition
General Election	election to choose all the House of Commons' 646 MPs
government	the group of ministers who decide on policies for running the country. These ministers come from the largest political party chosen by the people in a General Election.
head of state	the figure at the head of government. In some countries the head of state is a powerful position, in the UK it is held by the monarch, and is mainly a ceremonial position.
hereditary	passed on within a family, from one generation to the next
Home Office	the branch of government which administers law and order
human rights	the basic rights of an individual, e.g. freedom of speech
Industrial Revolution	a period in the 18th and 19th centuries when Britain moved from an economy based on farming to one based on industry

legislation	laws passed by Parliament
Loyalist	someone who supports the union of Northern Ireland and Great Britain
manifesto	a political party's proposals for running the country. It is put to the people before a general election.
Member of Parliament (MP)	someone elected to represent a constituency in the House of Commons
minister	a senior government figure who is responsible for a specific area of policy, for instance Minister of Defence
monarch	the king or queen
multi-cultural	a society made up of people from a wide variety of cultures and ethnic groups
Nationalist	In UK politics, someone opposed to the union between Northern Ireland and Great Britain
opposition	the second largest political party in the parliament
parliament	the elected assembly that represents the people in a democracy
parliamentary session	the period during which Parliament sits
party	a large group of people who broadly share the same plans for how the country should be run
peer	a member of the House of Lords
political prisoner	anyone imprisoned for political acts or beliefs
politician	someone whose main career is in politics
proportional representation (PR)	an electoral system under which seats are allocated to parties in proportion to the percentage of votes they receive
Protestant	a member of a Christian Church separate from the Roman Catholic Church which follows the principles of the Reformation
Radical	a nineteenth century politician who wanted to make dramatic changes to how the country was governed
referendum	a direct vote by the electorate of a country about a specific issue
republic	a country without a monarch
Republican	in Northern Ireland, one who wants a united Ireland
rights	the entitlements of a citizen, for instance the right to vote
royal assent	the formal signing of an Act of Parliament by the monarch
shadow Cabinet	senior figures in the opposition who hold titles similar to government ministers, for instance the shadow Chancellor represents the opposition in areas under the control of the Chancellor of the Exchequer
strike	refusing to do something, usually work
taxation	the process by which money is raised to pay for government services
trade union	an association of workers who hope to protect their conditions
treaty	formal agreement between states
Unionist	someone in favour of keeping Northern Ireland within the UK
universal suffrage	the right of all adults to vote
visa	a document allowing entry into a foreign country

INDEX